D1302115

持眮色 埘藕動 乃拿大 渚此陪卅

CHINESE FOODS
AND RECIPES

持眮色 埘藕動 乃拿大 渚此陪卅

ERIN MAHER

The Rosen Publishing Group's
READING ROOM
Collection

New York

THE RECIPES IN THIS COOKBOOK ARE INTENDED FOR A CHILD TO MAKE TOGETHER WITH AN ADULT.

Published in 2003 by The Rosen Publishing Group, Inc.
29 East 21st Street, New York, NY 10010

First Library Edition 2003

Book Design: Ron A. Churley

Photo Credits: Cover, p. 1 © Image Port/Index Stock; pp. 4, 5, 12, 17 by Ron A. Churley; p. 7 © Margerin Studios, Inc./FPG International, Victor Scocozza/FPG International; p. 8 © Cliff Hollenbeck/International Stock Photo; pp. 9, 11, 15, 21 by Christine Innamorato; p. 10 © Kindra Clineff/Index Stock; pp. 12–13, 19 © TravelPix/FPG International; p. 14 © Great American Stock/Index Stock; p. 16 © Floyd Holdman/International Stock Photo; p. 19 © Keren Su/FPG International; p. 20 © Peter Gridley/FPG International; p. 22 © SuperStock.

Library of Congress Cataloging-in-Publication Data

Maher, Erin, 1971-
   Chinese foods and recipes / author, Erin Maher.
      p. cm. — (The Rosen Publishing Group's reading room collection)
Summary: Discusses the history and traditions of China by focusing on
its foods and recipes.
   ISBN 0-8239-3748-8
   1. Cookery, Chinese—Juvenile literature. 2. Food
habits—China—Juvenile literature. [1. Cookery, Chinese. 2. Food
habits—China. 3. China—Social life and customs.] I. Title. II.
Series.
   TX724.5.C5 M275 2002
   641.5951—dc21
                                        2001007174

Manufactured in the United States of America

For More Information
Really Cookin' – Kids' Recipes – China
http://www2.whirlpool.com/html/homelife/cookin/krecchina.htm

Chinese New Year: Chinese Recipes
http://www.web-holidays.com/lunar/chfood.htm#cake

CONTENTS

A LOOK AT CHINA

China is a country in eastern Asia. It is the third largest country on Earth. Only Russia and Canada are larger. More than 1 billion people live in China. That's about one-fifth of all the people in the world! More people live in China than in any other country on Earth.

China's land includes deserts, tall mountains, and rich farmland. More than half of

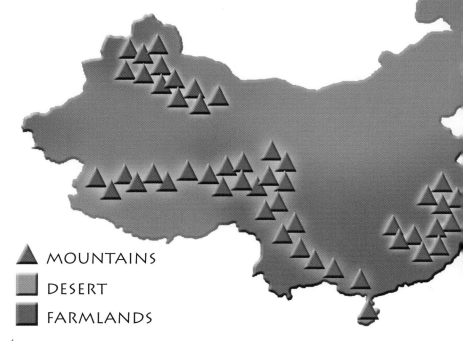

▲ MOUNTAINS
■ DESERT
■ FARMLANDS

China's workers are farmers. China produces more rice and tea than any other country in the world. It is also one of the leading producers of wheat, cotton, peanuts, and corn.

China's history goes back nearly 4,000 years. It is one of the oldest **civilizations** (sih-vuh-lih-ZAY-shunz) in the world. Over hundreds of years, countries like Japan and Korea have borrowed from Chinese language, **religion**, and art.

ASIA

CHINA

China is so large that it covers more than one-fifth of Asia, the world's largest continent. China has almost four times as many people as the United States!

A CHINESE MEAL

Many countries have borrowed from Chinese cooking. Chinese food is one of the world's great cooking styles. The Chinese consider cooking a form of art, and present food in beautiful and fancy ways.

In the south, rice is usually eaten during every meal, including breakfast. People in the north eat more wheat, which they make into noodles. The Chinese eat a lot of vegetables, like cabbage and mushrooms, and tofu (TOH-foo), which is made from **soybeans**. A Chinese meal might include vegetables, meat or seafood, rice or noodles, and soup. **Ginger**, bamboo shoots, and water chestnuts are also often used. Bamboo shoots come from the bamboo plant, a giant woody grass that grows throughout China. Water chestnuts come from the bulbs of plants that grow in flooded fields.

The Chinese take pride in the way their food is presented. They sometimes display food in the shape of flowers, or even in the form of animals, like roosters or dragons.

Because rice makes up such a large part of the Chinese diet, people cook it in different ways. Sometimes they steam rice and serve it with vegetables and meat or seafood. Sometimes they fry rice with meat

A special pot called a wok is used in making fried rice.

and vegetables. You may have had fried rice in a Chinese restaurant.

A cooking pot called a wok is important in Chinese cooking. A wok looks like a big metal bowl. It is used to cook dishes that contain meat, vegetables, and rice. The meat and rice are usually cooked first. Vegetables are added when the meal is almost cooked. This helps keep them crisp and helps keep their bright colors and healthy **vitamins**.

FRIED RICE

YOU WILL NEED:

3 tbsps. peanut oil
4 cups boiled rice, cold
1 tsp. salt
1/2 tsp. black pepper
1/2 green pepper,
    chopped
1/2 cup mushrooms,
    sliced
1/4 cup water
    chestnuts, sliced
1/2 cup bean sprouts
1/4 cup green onion,
    chopped
3 eggs, beaten
1/2 cup parsley,
    chopped

HOW TO DO IT:

Heat oil in a wok or skillet over high heat. Add rice and fry until hot, stirring constantly. Stir in salt and pepper.

Add green pepper, mushrooms, water chestnuts, bean sprouts, and green onion. Continue stirring. Push mixture to the sides of the wok or skillet, making an empty space in the center. Pour eggs into the empty space and let cook halfway through. Blend eggs into the rice mixture. Heat until eggs are fully cooked. Remove from heat. Sprinkle chopped parsley over each serving. Serves 4 to 6.

9

In many countries around the world, food is eaten one course, or dish, at a time. In China, all the different dishes are usually served at the same time. Many people in China eat soup at the end of the meal rather than at the beginning. People eat desserts only on special occasions.

Chinese people use **chopsticks** instead of forks and knives. Chopsticks are long, thin sticks made from the strong stem of the bamboo plant.

A person holds the chopsticks in one hand and uses them to scoop up food from a bowl or plate.

Have you ever used chopsticks? It takes some practice, but using chopsticks can be fun!

CHICKEN EGG-DROP SOUP

YOU WILL NEED:

4 cups chicken broth
1 tbsp. cornstarch
1 egg
3 tbsps. green onion,
     chopped

HOW TO DO IT:

Bring broth to a boil in a large pot over medium-high heat. Reduce heat to simmer. Mix cornstarch with a few drops of water. Stir into the broth. Beat egg in a bowl with a fork. Pour the egg into the soup, stirring constantly. Cook for 2 minutes or until egg is cooked and looks like scrambled eggs. Sprinkle with green onion. Serves 4.

ALL AROUND CHINA

The different **regions** of China have their own special styles of cooking. The city of **Beijing** (bay-ZHING) is in northern China. Beijing is the capital of China. For many years, the **emperors** of China lived in Beijing. The emperors wanted great food for their meals, so the food had to be very special. Beijing duck is a well-known dish that is still cooked in northern China. The duck is eaten with thin pancakes and a sweet sauce made from soybeans.

BEIJING

The northern part of China does not get as much rain as other parts of the country, so rice is not grown there. People who live in northern China usually eat noodles, **dumplings**, and thin pancakes with their meat and vegetables.

A special meal at the emperor's palace might include several hundred courses!

13

Egg rolls and sweet and sour dishes are prepared in the Cantonese style. A Cantonese dish called Mu Shu Pork sometimes contains lily buds!

You may have tasted an egg roll at a Chinese restaurant. An egg roll is a mixture of vegetables and bits of meat inside a fried crust. Egg rolls come from the city of **Canton** (kan-TAHN) in the south of China. The Chinese name for Canton means "city of goats." People in the United States and around the world are most familiar with the Cantonese (kan-tuh-NEEZ) style of cooking, which uses mild spices. Cantonese food is served in most Chinese restaurants.

People who live in Canton eat a lot of seafood—like fish, shrimp, crab, and lobster—because their city is close to the South China Sea.

CANTONESE SWEET AND SOUR PORK

YOU WILL NEED:

1/2 cup flour
1/2 tsp. salt
1/2 tsp. black pepper
1 lb. lean pork loin, cut
    in bite-sized pieces
3 tbsps. peanut or
    vegetable oil
2 green peppers, cut in
    large pieces
1 onion, sliced
1 carrot, sliced
1/2 cup pineapple
    chunks
1/4 cup white vinegar
2 tbsps. soy sauce
1/2 cup pineapple juice
1/4 cup brown
    sugar
2 tbsps. cornstarch
Few drops red food
    coloring

HOW TO DO IT:

Mix flour, salt, and pepper in a plastic bag. Add pork pieces. Shake bag well to coat each piece. Remove pork and throw away bag. Heat oil in a large frying pan. Brown pork pieces on all sides. Lower heat and cook for 20 minutes. Add peppers, onion, and carrot. Fry for 5 minutes. Stir in remaining ingredients. Cook until mixture is hot. Serve over cooked rice. Serves 4 to 5.

The Yangtze River is the world's third longest river.

The **Szechwan** (SESH-WAHN) region is in the central part of China. One of the world's longest rivers, the **Yangtze** (YANG-SEE), runs through this region. The Yangtze River is over 3,900 miles long. This is farther than the distance from New York to California!

The weather in the Szechwan region is warm and humid, which is perfect for growing rice. Szechwan food is known for being very spicy. If you order a Szechwan dish at a Chinese restaurant, it will be very hot. Szechwan cooking uses hot peppers, green onions, ginger, soy sauce, garlic, and **sesame** (SEH-suh-mee) oil to flavor the food.

16

CHINESE NOODLES IN PEANUT SAUCE

YOU WILL NEED:

1 lb. spaghetti or
  fettuccini
1/2 cup dark sesame oil
6 tbsps. peanut butter
1/4 cup water
3 tbsps. light soy sauce
6 tbsps. dark soy sauce
6 tbsps. sesame paste
  (tahini)
4 tsps. rice wine vinegar
1/4 cup honey
4 medium garlic cloves,
  minced
2 tsps. fresh ginger,
  minced (or 1 1/4
  tsps. ground ginger)
1 tbsp. hot pepper oil

HOW TO DO IT:

Cook spaghetti in a large pot of boiling water over medium heat for about 9 minutes. Spaghetti should still be a bit firm. Drain. Rinse with cold water. Drain again. Toss spaghetti with 2 tbsps. dark sesame oil. Combine remaining sesame oil and the rest of the ingredients in a blender and blend until smooth. Thin mixture with hot water to the consistency of whipped cream. Just before serving, toss spaghetti with sauce. Garnish with cucumber, peanuts, and green onion, if desired. Serves 6.

FESTIVALS AND FOOD

Chinese people around the world use food as a part of their celebrations. The dinner on the night before the Chinese New Year is very important. Families get together to share a special meal. In northern China, dumplings are served for good luck. The meal might also include dried oysters and seaweed.

The Chinese New Year celebration lasts for several days and begins between January 21 and February 19. Some people celebrate for up to a month! Families decorate their houses with red paper designs. The Chinese believe that red is the color of good luck. Fireworks are used to chase away evil spirits and welcome the new year. On the last night of the celebration, some people dress in dragon costumes to amuse the children.

People begin planning the Chinese New Year celebration weeks before the festival even starts.

Chinese people have celebrated the Mid-Autumn Festival for almost 700 years.

Every year, Chinese people all over the world celebrate the full moon and the coming of autumn during the Mid-Autumn Festival in September. This is also sometimes called the Moon Festival. Families come together and eat sweets called mooncakes, just as Chinese people have done for hundreds of years. Mooncakes are small, round cakes that are usually filled with a sweet paste. Their round shape stands for families coming together to spend time with each other. The cakes may contain fruit, nuts, or other fillings. Rice pudding is also eaten on special occasions.

RICE PUDDING

YOU WILL NEED:

3/4 cup rice
1 1/2 cups water
pinch of salt
4 cups milk
1/2 cup sugar
1/2 tsp. vanilla extract

HOW TO DO IT:

Combine rice, water, and salt in a large pot. Heat until almost boiling, stirring often. Lower heat, cover pot, and simmer for 15 minutes or until most of the water is gone. Stir in the milk and the sugar. Cook uncovered for 30 to 40 minutes or until mixture is thick and creamy, stirring often. Stir in vanilla. Serve topped with sliced almonds, whipped cream, or a sprinkle of cinnamon. Serves 6.

CHINESE COOKING IN AMERICA

Many Chinese people have moved to the United States over the last 100 years. They have brought their cooking styles with them.

These cooking styles have changed over time because it was difficult for Chinese American people to get some of the ingredients they needed in the United States. Many dishes that we think of as Chinese were actually created by mixing Chinese and American cooking styles. Even fortune cookies were created by Chinese Americans. In China, they call these cookies "American fortune cookies"!

GLOSSARY

Beijing The capital city of China.

Canton A city in southern China.

chopsticks A pair of thin sticks made from the bamboo plant that people use to eat food.

civilization A culture that has a system of writing and keeps written records.

dumpling A round piece of dough that is boiled or steamed and is often filled with meat.

emperor The ruler of a large territory called an empire.

ginger A spice made from the root of a plant.

region An area.

religion A system of faith in which a god or gods are honored.

sesame The small seeds of a plant that can be made into an oil or a paste used in many Chinese dishes.

soybean A bean that is widely used as a source of food in Asia.

Szechwan An area of central China known for its spicy cooking.

vitamin One of many special chemicals in food that the body needs to work properly.

Yangtze The longest river in China.

INDEX